*The School System Comparison
Between the United States of America
and Finland*

What are the differences? Why does Finns score higher on international tests?

Why cannot the American students apply their knowledge in real life situations— or can they?

Innovative methods used at school

The Global Pandemic and Changes in Learning

Copyright © 2021 Anna Fielding, 2nd Edition
All rights reserved.

ISBN: 9798756134179

Contents

THE

FOREWORD..1

CHAPTER 1: THE BACKROUND: THE INTERNATIONAL ASSESSMENTS 6

CHAPTER 2: TWO ACTS: NO CHILD LEFT BEHIND AND THE AMERICAN RECOVER AND REINVESTMENT 10

CHAPTER 3: THE FINNISH SCHOOL SYSTEM IN A NUTSHELL..........................18

CHAPTER 4: FINLAND'S SCHOOL SYSTEM AND THE CLASS SIZE.................28

CHAPTER 5: MATHEMATICS 33

CHAPTER 6: READING LITERACY...........40

CHAPTER 7: SCIENCE 52

CHAPTER 8: STATEWIDE ASSESSMENTS 55

CHAPTER 9: OTHER DIFFERENCES AND SIMILARITIES...59

CHAPTER 10: SCHOOL LUNCHES – NOT JUST NURTITIONAL BUT ALSO EDUCATIONAL VALUES 65

CHAPTER 11: LANGUAGE, CULTURE, AND BUSINESS SKILLS 75

CHAPTER 12: INNOVATIVE IDEAS FOR A SCHOOL DAY 79

CHAPTER 13: MATHEMATICS – INNOVATIVE LEARNING METHODS.....82

CHAPTER 14: LANGUAGE LEARNING INNOVATIVE METHODS...........................87

CHAPTER 15: E-LEARNING: STUDENTS VS. TEACHERS 91

CHAPTER 16: GLOBAL PANDEMIC AND LEARNING CHALLENGES.........................94

CHAPTER 17: CONCLUSIONS....................99

ABOUT THE AUTHOR 105

SCHOOL SYSTEM COMPARISON BETWEEN THE UNITED STATES OF AMERICA AND FINLAND..........................I

WHY CANNOT THE AMERICAN STUDENTS APPLY THEIR KNOWLEDGE IN REAL LIFE SITUATIONS— OR CAN THEY? III

INNOVATIVE METHODS USED AT SCHOOL III

THE GLOBAL PANDEMIC AND CHANGES IN LEARNING III

FOREWORD

Educational issues have been discussed during the presidential campaign, the state elections, and especially after the global pandemic has changed the way the students learn: face-to-face, hybrid, or online.

The second edition of this book includes some innovative teaching ideas, and the Covid-19 concerns in socioeconomic level.

The School System Comparison Between the United States of America and Finland

The main concern is the state of education in the United States. And why does it differ from other countries?

Why do the American students score lower than many other countries in international tests?

Why are the American students not interested in science and mathematics? Why their scores are not as high?

This book discusses about the similarities and differences between two countries: Finland and the United States. Finland has scored high in all the international assessments, whereas the United States has not.

The low scores in international assessments are puzzling because the U.S. universities are top class, and therefore, you would expect the American students score high when compared the students aged fifteen. Instead, the American students score lower, and they have been scoring about the same level for the past decade.

Are the top universities only for rich and privileged students, and therefore, they have more possibilities to succeed and thrive, whereas these international tests are made among all the students?

This short book is written from the point of view of a former student. I have gone through the 12-year school system in Finland. My middle and high school were among the top two schools in

The School System Comparison Between the United States of America and Finland

Finland's nationwide school ranking at the time when I went to school there.

I am currently living in the United States, and I have observed the American school system in Michigan as a parent and an observer of some of the students. Therefore, the differences are subjective, and written from a point of view of one state. This includes just the first-10th grades of the U.S. school system.

First, I will discuss about the international assessments that have been widely discussed in the news and during the presidential campaign. These OECD's student assessments include mathematics, reading, and science literacy comparisons.

Secondly, I will discuss about the school system, the class sizes, and the similarities and differences when compared the American school system to Finland.

CHAPTER 1:

THE BACKROUND: THE

INTERNATIONAL ASSESSMENTS

Finland has been among the top countries in the international student assessments since the year 2000 whereas the United States has not reached the top level in years 2000 – 2009 reporting in mathematics, science, or literacy knowledge and skills.

The United States' score has been the same as the average score, or a little bit below or above of the average of the OECD-countries.

For some reason, the American students have more difficulty in using their knowledge in real life situations and problem solving.

Nevertheless, this result will also have an impact on the American's ability to compete in

The School System Comparison Between the United States of America and Finland

international markets if the education lacks behind or stays at the average level.

It can also reflect on the general interest of being educated: how many of these students will go to college/university, are dropouts, or only have a high school –diploma?

The education will reflect on their salary, societal class, and standard of living, their ability to buy things as consumers, what they can offer to their children in the future, and what they can expect to have as means of living when they retire. How many of these young adults consider their future as a means of income, societal level, their children, or their retirement? Few, if any.

CHAPTER 2: TWO ACTS: NO CHILD LEFT BEHIND AND THE AMERICAN RECOVER AND REINVESTMENT

The No Child Left Behind Act (NCLB) was introduced in 2001 and approve as a law with bipartisan support when the public was concerned about the condition of education.

In short, NCLB requires schools to have standardized tests, and assess basic skills. It requires accountability of schools and teachers of the state of education in schools in the United States.

According to several international studies, regardless of this One Child Left Behind –program, the United States has not done any better since this act was introduced.

Has this program made any difference in the state level?

The difference is that schools and teachers are now assessed, and they are accountable for the education. The assessment shows if some schools or teachers are below the average level. All children are supposed to get the same educational

The School System Comparison Between the United States of America and Finland

possibilities within a state where these statewide assessments are held.

However, this act has not changed the knowledge or skills when compared to other countries.

Moreover, just assessing the children does not make any difference how the children will use their knowledge and how they can use their knowledge in real life situations and problem solving.

Education, knowledge, and skills are important in gaining the competitive advantage over the other countries. They are also important in innovating.

Innovations are the basis of new patents that can create new jobs and new income. Innovations can also be process innovations, e.g. how things are done better, faster, or more cost-efficiently. That is why the American students need to learn to use their knowledge in real life situations and solve problems.

Thus, as the results in international tests show, there is no big difference in the U.S. education during the past decade, regardless of who has been the president, or who has had the majority in congress and in the senate. The whole education system and how it is assessed should be re-evaluated and renewed. The old way of thinking is not brining any benefits to the children at school.

The American Recover and Reinvestment Act has invested in education: early learning programs, including Head Start, Early Head Start, childcare, and programs for children with special needs, reforms to strengthen elementary and secondary education, and to stabilize state education budgets. This act also encourages states to improve teachers' effectiveness, assessments that will improve both teaching and learning. This act also aims to encourage innovation. Moreover, this act includes funds to address college affordability and improve access to higher education. [1]

The Race to the Top-Early Learning Challenge (RTT-ELC) is administered by the Departments of Education (ED) and Health and Human Services (HHS). It requires the states to develop high-quality early learning systems, which in turn will help to ensure that children entering schools are ready and able to succeed. [2]

Will any of these topics mentioned in this ARR - Act addresses the problem of the state of education in the United States when compared to other countries?

The School System Comparison Between the United States of America and Finland

Encouraging the innovation will assist in gaining competitive advantage if innovations are created.

In addition, improving access to higher education or college education will improve the general state of education in the United States. It will not change the comparison results among the 15-year-olds. The early learning programs might help, but it is too early to say.

REFERENCES

1 www.whitehouse.gov/issues/education, retrieved June 2, 2012

2 www.ed.gov/blog/2011/05/rtt-early-learning-challenge, retrieved June 2, 2012.

CHAPTER 3: THE FINNISH SCHOOL SYSTEM IN A NUTSHELL

This chapter describes the Finnish school system briefly. The Finnish school system includes the elementary school – just like the U.S. school system, and the middle school, and the high school (three years).

The high school grades are also called the upper classes of the secondary school.

The matriculation examination is the final exam after the three high school years.

The term **matriculation examination** refers to educational qualifications in Finland and how well the students have learned the skills and gained knowledge in the topics taught at school.

The students are encouraged to use their knowledge in real life situations and solve problems.

About the Finnish Matriculation Examination: it was first arranged in Finland in 1852. In the beginning, the examination was the entrance

The School System Comparison Between the United States of America and Finland

examination to Helsinki University, and then the student had to show sufficient evidence of an all-round education and knowledge of Latin.

Today, no Latin is required, however, it is still important when considering a higher education.

Passing the Matriculation Examination entitles the student to continue his or her studies at university. The results of this examination form a part of the points calculated and assessed when applied to a university or to a college. In some cases, excellent grades can get you directly into a university.

The Matriculation Examination is held biannually, in spring and in autumn, in all Finnish upper secondary schools/high schools, at the same time. All the students need to have the similar possibilities to pass the test, have the same time, and the same questions so that every student answers the same questions on the exact same day/time to avoid cheating and leaking the answers beforehand.

The purpose of the examination is to find out the level of knowledge and skills the students have acquired based on the curriculum for the upper secondary school/high school, and if the students have reached an adequate level of maturity in their educational goals.

The examination is arranged in all the schools.

The School System Comparison Between the United States of America and Finland

The Matriculation Examination Board is responsible for the guidelines of the exam, administering the examination, its arrangements, assessments, and execution. The Ministry of Education nominates the chair of the Board and its forty members, and these board members represent the various subjects covered by the Matriculation Examination. Several hundred associate members and employees assist the members in the preparation, administration, assessment, and they take care of the technical arrangements.

A student must complete the examination during the three consecutive examination periods, or it can also be completed in one examination period.

Each student can decide if he wants to take the examination in one period or in several.

There are benefits in both.

If you take the examination in one period, you can apply to universities earlier if you pass the examination. But if you take the examination during several periods (maximum amount is three periods), then you can study more, learn more, and possibly get a better grade.

Some Finnish schools offer the **International Baccalaureate Diploma Program (IBDP)** which is a two-year educational program for 16–19-aged students. It is an internationally accepted

The School System Comparison Between the United States of America and Finland

qualification for entry into higher education, and it is supposedly recognized by universities worldwide.

However, not all the universities will accept or recognize the grades or the studies as they have their own qualifications and curriculums to follow. It can be hard to prove that you have valid knowledge and skills in a particular topic when the receiving university does not have the same configuration of studies, or even same areas of studies. More often, the receiving university will require extra studies to prove that the transferring student is qualified.

Some high schools highlight language skills, some mathematics, some art, and some physical education. These special high schools are usually only for the best of the best students, the ones who show the most potential in these areas. The students are allowed to excel in their topic and learn above the requirements of the normal high school level.

For instance, if you go to a school that offers foreign languages, you can start the first foreign language at third grade. Swedish is the mandatory second domestic language in Finland and that is usually the new language, unless your family is Swedish speaking, and then you can choose one of the other languages, for instance, English, French, German or Russian languages.

The School System Comparison Between the United States of America and Finland

In the fifth grade, you can start the second foreign language, usually English.

The seventh graders take on French, German or Russian or some other language.

There is also a possibility to begin learning a fourth language at the eighth grade. (French, German, Russian or some other language). As well as fifth and/or sixth languages in high school.

For instance, I started studying the English language on in the second grade, the Swedish language in the fifth grade and the French on seventh grade, and then the German language on the tenth grade. Therefore, I had four foreign languages at school.

This gave me basic skills and knowledge of these languages. It is also considered to be a competitive advantage: the more languages you know, the more possibilities you can have to get a job.

In addition, the cultural differences of France, Germany, Russia, and other countries are taught at school during the language studies, and therefore, you will be more knowledgeable of the cultures that you will enter and do business with when you have some knowledge of it.

CHAPTER 4: FINLAND'S SCHOOL SYSTEM AND THE CLASS SIZE

This chapter discusses about the importance of the class size because this topic has been lately in all the recent presidential and governmental campaign topics. This is because Finland had received top scores on international tests in several years. Something in that school system works.

In Finland, the class size varies from 12 – 36 students.

I had classes with just ten to twelve students, especially in language studies.

The advantage is that the teacher can concentrate on each student and their progress more intensively. Whereas, in classes of thirty-six students, each student is considered equal, and the teaching is standardized for the whole class, no time for individual teaching.

However, both class sizes have their benefits. First, even if you have a small class, you can have students that do not need individual coaching.

They might all be at the same level or progress the same pace and then it is just a waste of teaching resources to have a small class.

The School System Comparison Between the United States of America and Finland

With thirty-six students, you can give the basic lessons, homework, and tests, and based on the results you will see which students' progress well and which ones do not.

Usually, the small classes in Finland are either in subjects, which were not so popular, or in scarcely populated areas.

If you start a small class for a specific topic, like for instance learning Italian or Chinese language, and assign a teacher for this class, there is always a problem, that some students drop out during the school year or lose their interest in learning this subject, and then you have too small a class to continue with the other students. It is a waste of resources unless this same teacher can teach other topics as well.

Some schools have opted for teachers that can teach a specific language and some other language, like for instance, French and Germany. However, it is not always easy to find teachers capable of teaching several subjects.

However, the students might be interested in learning diverse topics.

As a summary, offering a variety of subjects, you might get the students to stay at school and improve their skills.

The School System Comparison Between the United States of America and Finland

However, the fact is that special needs children do need individualized attention. You cannot do that if your class size is larger, twenty to thirty-six students. You need a different approach: you need a smaller class size. You need an individual approach and time to follow up each task.

The basic subjects like mathematics, reading, and science are larger classes than any other topic at any school. Normally the class size in these topics varies from 20 – 336 students in class. Therefore, the current debate if the class size is important, it is not that important.

CHAPTER 5: MATHEMATICS

Mathematics is always important. Whatever you do in life and whatever is your profession you will need mathematics skills.

The term mathematics here means algebra, geometry, calculus, analyses, combinatorics, dynamical systems and differentiations, logic, computation, probability, and statistics

The School System Comparison Between the United States of America and Finland

It does not matter if you will be a homemaker, a teacher, a restaurant worker, or a manager, you will need mathematics skills. Therefore, it is utmost important to teach mathematics and make sure that the students understand the value of learning mathematics skills. The importance of mathematics in different areas of life and in different workplaces is not stressed enough. Mathematics should be introduced as the most important skill you can have when you graduate.

The major difference in mathematics teaching between Finland and the United States is not what is taught, but when the different topics are being taught.

When I was at the elementary school, I had to learn my adding and subtracting and multiplication tables during the first and the second grade.

In Michigan, the students learn the multiplication tables during the third-fourth grades. But this shows that it is later than in Finland which is the comparison country in this short study.

I do not know if this is same with other states.

You need to be fluent with your multiplication tables, you're adding, and subtracting skills otherwise if you don't' learn these during the first

The School System Comparison Between the United States of America and Finland

grades at school, you will always struggle with them later. It is the basis of your mathematics skills. If you cheat and do not memorize your tables, then you will always waste your time later when you need to add, subtract, or multiply or divide faster.

In addition, dividing numbers were taught later in Michigan schools than what I had learned in Finnish schools.

Is there too much repetition in earlier grades at U.S. schools, so that there is no time to learn these skills earlier?

Nevertheless, later when you go to middle school and high school, the teaching catches up and the Finns and the Americans learn about the same issues about the same age.

Probabilities were taught a year earlier in the schools in the United States of America than what I had in Finnish schools.

In Finnish schools, if the teacher had time, they would explain these during the ninth-grade spring semester, but otherwise they would be taught in the tenth grade. However, there are differences in this between schools and states.

The School System Comparison Between the United States of America and Finland

Mathematics exercises seem to be about the same in the United States of America. as in Finnish schools.

Sometimes, it seems that the American teachers do not give enough homework for students but does exercises at school.

However, if you do the exercises at school, you do not know if all the students are following or if they are just daydreaming during the class. Nevertheless, there are differences between schools and teaching methods.

Moreover, the most memorable teachers in mathematics were those who managed to connect the topic to something concrete, a real-life issue, for example why you need to learn to add and subtract? Because every time you buy something, you need to know how much change you will get back and how much money you have left.

Also, in more difficult mathematics topics, connecting differentiation, a rate of change, to a real-life example, to business and economics.

It makes more sense to students when they consider a real-life business or financial problem, than just learn the theory.

CHAPTER 6: READING LITERACY

Reading literacy is usually reached when you are 5-7 years old in Finland, and children usually can read when they go to first grade or learn it during that grade.

The reading lessons are similar in the U.S. and in Finland: you encourage children to read books that interest them and then ask them to write about these books.

Fielding

What I found was that one of the differences between Finland and Michigan elementary schools was that in Michigan, you did not compose essays, fairy tales, or fantasy stories in any grade.

The only writing exercises what I saw were: telling about your summer activities, or what would you give to your mother as a gift, or something similar, noticeably short essays, which did not require very much imagination.

I remember having written essays since the first grade and more imaginative stories later when I was at the second grade and all the way to the sixth grade. The teachers encouraged to use the language

The School System Comparison Between the United
States of America and Finland

and write either fictional or factual stories. It was part of the curriculum.

In the middle school, you were also asked to write about certain topics.

For instance, eight grade writing skills could include writing about topics like the school transformation in the digital age, writing an opinion about a news topic, traffic development in your city and what would you do to change it, find new innovative ways to use an old, abandoned factory, and writing a letter imagining to be someone else (for example a former president writing to his wife or giving a speech addressing the nation).

Some of these skills, like writing a letter, and analyzing a book and drafting an essay about it, are included in the curriculum at schools in the United State of America, too.

The difference in writing homework was the length: in Michigan nineth grade, the teachers required five-paragraph essay about a book, whereas when I was at school, the requirement were usually three to four pages, if you wanted a good grade (A, B).

It is good to give an exact paragraph number for homework, and then everyone knows what is

The School System Comparison Between the United States of America and Finland

expected. It is the basically same as if they had given the number of pages to write.

However, number of paragraphs was less than three to four pages. And, thus, it seems that the children in Michigan schools are required less than what children in Finnish schools, and that could explain the differences in learning and knowledge.

One difference that I noticed was that we drafted more essays during the school year than what the students did in any grade in Michigan.

We had about one to two essays/month. Essay writing showed the progress of the student: the grammar, the spelling skills, the plot and characterization in fiction/fairy tales, and the narrative skills.

The teacher was able to detect the problem areas and put more emphasis on teaching and discussing these areas.

What I noticed as a problem with some students in Michigan during the third to fifth grades was that they did not understand if the story was a fiction or not.

In addition, they had a hard time following a plot and remembering the characters of the book.

Somehow, these students did not understand that a fiction book was like a new world and every

The School System Comparison Between the United States of America and Finland

time you started a new book, you opened a window to a new world, a world that was different in all the books. These students only picked up some details of the story but did not understand what was said.

They just read one chapter after another, word after word, without grasping what they were reading.

They had the reading and the spelling skills, but not the skill to comprehend their reading and imagine the fantasy world. Thus, they had a difficult time retrieving information or understand the feelings and reasoning of the characters and their actions.

Our teacher in Finland also encouraged us to read books at home, just like in Michigan schools.

It was also more competitive than in Michigan elementary or middle schools because the teachers tracked and informed the students how many books, they all had read in a week or in a month and this was followed during the whole school year.

Even if it encouraged the competition in reading, it also encouraged the students less enthusiastic in reading to participate and read books.

The similarities in reading and writing classes included reading short stories, analyzing poems, and

The School System Comparison Between the United
States of America and Finland

discussing about them. In Finland, the short stories and poems were also read and discussed in foreign language classes.

In English classes, there were a lot more spelling quizzes and tests in Michigan than what I ever had at school.

It took a lot of time in the elementary school just to quiz the spelling of different words. That was one difference between the school system that some things you are expected to learn by yourself in Finland, and these are then taught and repeated here in U.S. classes.

English is more difficult in spelling and writing than Finnish language. The spelling skill is necessary. However, the question is how much time do you need to spend quizzing the spelling of the words during the school hours and how much can you expect the children to learn by themselves?

I think in Finland, the students were expected to learn more at home than what was expected in Michigan today.

However, this is not part of the problem.

The problem is still the same: the students need to learn to use their imagination, use their knowledge in a real-life situation and be creative.

The School System Comparison Between the United States of America and Finland

This was not taught in Michigan schools.

Overall, the teaching has the same puzzle pieces in both countries: reading short stories, grammar, reading articles, reading fiction books, reading nonfiction, reading poems, drafting essays, analyzing text, and answering questions about the text.

Nevertheless, they are not taught during the same grades or with the same emphasis in these two countries.

Fielding

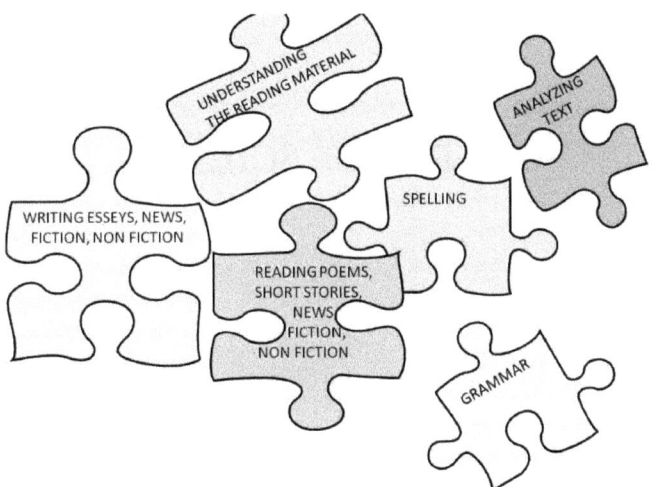

CHAPTER 7: SCIENCE

The science lessons are different in the United States than in Finland.

In Finland, you study biology, geography, chemistry, and physics whereas in the United States you study biology and science.

The elementary school level is about the same in both countries, but then when the students reach the middle school and high school, it differs.

Chemistry and physics are taught during seventh – ninth grade in Finland.

In high school, you can choose if you want to study more of mathematics, physics, and chemistry or more languages, or something else. It depends on your skills and what your career plans are what you study.

There are some basic skills and lesions that you need to learn even if you choose languages, for example, instead of mathematics. You will still study mathematics but not as many hours as someone who has chosen mathematics, chemistry, and physics as their primary interests.

The U.S. middle grade and high school teaches biology in more detail to all the students than what

The School System Comparison Between the United
States of America and Finland

is required in Finland, for instance, I never had to dissect an animal, or learn all the bones. But there are differences between schools.

The similarities include, for instance, learning about the osmosis, DNA, trees, and plants.

CHAPTER 8: STATEWIDE ASSESSMENTS

This chapter discusses of the other differences in school systems about statewide testing.

In the United States of America, many states have the state level testing and assessing the schools, the teachers, and education.

In Michigan this was called the MEAP test.

The government was able to rank the schools and teachers based on the MEAP test results.

The School System Comparison Between the United States of America and Finland

Also, the government was able to see if some school got poor grades year after year and take an action to correct the situation.

The MEAP test, or statewide testing, was designed to assure that all students across the state received the same training and evaluated on the same subject matter.

The MEAP tests are criterion-reference, meaning that students' results are assessed, compared, and reported against a set performance standard.

If a student meets the standard, it means he meets expectations on the recommended state curriculum.

In Finland, we do not have a yearly nationwide testing in nationwide or even in municipality level.

We do have a nationwide test in societal issues, like how well do you know our government, the society, the economy, and so on. Usually, the best student at the school gets a prize as well as the best student nationwide.

This nationwide test is held during the ninth grade.

Otherwise, the nationwide testing is just the matriculation examination which is nationwide.

The School System Comparison Between the United States of America and Finland

Of course, the teachers know what level of knowledge the students need to have to pass the matriculation examination.

CHAPTER 9: OTHER DIFFERENCES AND SIMILARITIES

This chapter discusses of the other differences in school systems.

In Finland, we do not have any snow days. You go to school regardless of snow or ice.

In addition, there is more snow in Finland than there is in Southern and Western Michigan due to the long winter season.

The School System Comparison Between the United States of America and Finland

However, north of Michigan has probably as much snow as there usually comes in Finland.

In Finland, students use the public transportation, walk, ride a bike, or are transported by their parents to school. In the United States, the students usually use the school buses.

In the United States, the school hours are usually from 8.30 a.m. to three p.m.

In Finland, the hours vary based on the school and what the curriculum is. Usually, school starts around 8-10 am and ends between one to four p.m.

This also depends on the grade. In high school, you can have more flexibility in when you go to school and when your school day ends, because it also depends on the classes you have chosen. Not all the students have the same classes.

For example, you can have ten a.m. to two p.m. days and then you can have nine am to three p.m. days and you can have eight a.m. to four p.m. days. You can also have "empty hours" during your school day due to your individual class schedule. This means that you can go home, do your homework during these hours when there are no school classes assigned.

In Finland, you can also have extra curriculum activities and extra classes after the normal school hours. These might be, for example, art classes.

The School System Comparison Between the United States of America and Finland

Both countries offer tutoring, counseling services for students, and career advises and visits to real workplaces.

The United States assesses teaching, students, and school every year with the statewide assessment tests. In Michigan, this was called the MEAP test.

In Finland, you do not assess the teaching and students every year. The matriculation examination in 12th grade in all the high schools in Finland assesses the students and their knowledge in different topics.

The examination questions are the same to all the students, all the schools, and are held at the same time in every single school.

The teachers do evaluate the students during their tenth to twelfth grade with the previous years' matriculation examination questions so that the students and the teachers know their skills and level. Nevertheless, it is not mandatory testing. It is good for the students and the teachers to know the level of knowledge so that there are no surprises when the actual examination results are revealed.

The school year starts two weeks later in the United States than in Finland.

In addition, the schools in the United States have a spring vacation in March-April, which does not exist in Finland, but instead there is a winter vacation in February for one week in Finland. In Finland, we also have an Easter vacation from

The School System Comparison Between the United States of America and Finland

Thursday to Monday during Easter holidays. The school ends May 31st in Finland, whereas many American schools end in June.

CHAPTER 10: SCHOOL LUNCHES – NOT JUST NURTITIONAL BUT ALSO EDUCATIONAL VALUES

This chapter discusses of the importance of school lunches, and healthy food choices.

There is a big difference in schools when compared Finland and the United States. In Finland, school lunch has been free for all the students since 1948.

The School System Comparison Between the United States of America and Finland

The parents pay the school food indirectly in their taxes, but they do not have to provide the food for their children to take with to school every morning.

This free school lunch means a healthy lunch. This lunch includes salad, milk or orange or other juice to drink, and a hot meal like for instance meat, fish, or pasta, and dessert, for instance fruits, berries, or something else. In addition, bread and butter/margarine is available.

The healthy lunch is important because you cannot study with empty stomach. One third of the daily energy needs should come from the lunch food.

Many students do not eat school food, or they eat only part of their portion.

Some students want only veggie food, and do not eat meat, and a veggie choice is not always possible to arrange in all the schools.

In the United States, there are children who do not get any food or truly little food at home, and they rely on the food they get at school; thus it is important, that the food at school is of good nutritional value and healthy.

Sometimes the students complain about the monotony of the food choices, and that the presentation of the food is not always so attractive. You need to present the food so that the students will try the food (even healthy food).

The School System Comparison Between the United States of America and Finland

The school lunch in Finland costs is the following: the ingredients costs about $0,70 - $0,86 but the whole lunch about $2,48– $3 per student per day. This was in 2012.

However, in January 2020, the average cost of a school meal was 2.80 euros (3.08 dollars) per day. [1]

The inflation has not changed it that much during the past nine years. However, with more children wanting special meals like vegetarian or special style meals (Mexican, Organic, etc.), the meal is likely to cost more. However, when the average price is around three dollars, the cheapest meal is only 64 euros (0.71 dollars).[2]

It is not that much but it is not cheap either.

The school food is paid by the government, not by the individual parents. The price depends on the school district and how they choose and assess their suppliers. Some schools compete better, and some do not.

In addition, the availability of suppliers deducts the price of the school food.

The good meal planning is essential to keep the cost down.[3]

The school lunch is also considered educational. When you can offer new experiences and introduce new meals, it will educate the students. Some students have never tried the traditional foods at home, some meals are more international, and thus, more interesting for the students to try.

The School System Comparison Between the United States of America and Finland

Furthermore, you can teach students the proper habits, for instance, the use of fork, knife, and spoon in different situations etc.

In addition, allergy choices are available, if you have informed the school kitchen about your allergies.

There are veggie days in schools, but these days have not yet been immensely popular according to the surveys among students. In capital city area, the schools have one veggie meal day/ week.

The most favorite school foods based on the surveys among the students were: lasagna, macaroni casserole with hamburger, spinach pancakes, meatballs, hamburger gravy (with either spaghetti or potatoes), potato-meat casserole, and fish sticks.

The school food can include more exotic choices to make the students see what other cultures can offer, for example, like Mexican, Thai, or Chinese food.

The traditional food of the country is important so that the children will learn and eat what has been traditionally served in Finnish tables for centuries. Many parents are so busy that they do not have time or skills to make these traditional foods, and therefore, school lunch might be the only place where the children will get these. In addition, today, there are many multicultural families which have different cultural and food traditions, and therefore,

The School System Comparison Between the United States of America and Finland

it is also an important role for school to show and offer different dishes.

However, it is not just the school lunch time that offers this traditional food information, but also the cooking and nutrition lessons offered at school during the 8-ninth grade.

And during the summer, when the school is closed, the government and the cities have tried the free lunch program in the parks.

This Park feeding program has proven to be successful.[4]

I remember having a free lunch at a playground in 1960s, so that idea is not a new one. It has been around for decades. The food might be just a pea soup with bread, but it is tasty and fills your stomach.

The School System Comparison Between the United States of America and Finland

References

1 Finland's cheapest school meal costs just 64 cents per day, January 10,2020, Yle, Retrieved 10/27/2021 from yle.fi/uutiset/osasto/news/finlands_cheapest_school_meal_costs_just_64_cents_per_day/11152708

2 Finland's cheapest school meal costs just 64 cents per day, January 10,2020, Yle, Retrieved 10/27/2021 from yle.fi/uutiset/osasto/news/finlands_cheapest_school_meal_costs_just_64_cents_per_day/11152708

3 Finland's cheapest school meal costs just 64 cents per day, January 10,2020, Yle, Retrieved 10/27/2021 from yle.fi/uutiset/osasto/news/finlands_cheapest_school_meal_costs_just_64_cents_per_day/11152708

4 Finland's free park lunch programmes spread in summer 2019, Yle, Retrieved 10/27/2021 from yle.fi/uutiset/osasto/news/finlands_free_park_lunch_programmes_spread_in_summer_2019/10827534

CHAPTER 11: LANGUAGE, CULTURE, AND BUSINESS SKILLS

I have heard some comments of how the American's do not understand the importance of culture and habits when doing business with other countries.

This is not a fact, because some of the American companies have excelled in their global business.

The School System Comparison Between the United States of America and Finland

However, it might be true when considering small businesses trying to expand abroad for the first time.

The language and culture can be a barrier for small businesses due to the basic education they received at school, but also the lack of different languages and learning different cultures at school.

When considering competitive advantage over the other countries, small businesses are also important.

Small businesses can create new jobs and become global companies if they have the knowledge, skills, funding, and good products and services to offer.

I would offer more training possibilities for small businesses, for instance: language courses, training in cultural issues and habits of foreign countries.

Even large companies can fail when trying to establish a market in a new country if they do not consider the culture and what people like. Therefore, I would also consider offering information of laws in different countries: how to hire and where to hire new employees, what are the working hours for minors, overtime, etc.

If you are not capable of embedding your business into a new society and make it visible and likable, your business will not succeed.

The School System Comparison Between the United States of America and Finland

Michigan had an excellent approach in teaching marketing during the ninth grade asking the students to draw a marketing campaign and then they discuss about the brand marketing.

It is important to add business skills to classes so that the students learn and understand what and why they need certain skills and knowledge.

This was just one example what one school did in Michigan, and there are many other examples of what teachers can do to increase business knowledge.

CHAPTER 12: INNOVATIVE IDEAS FOR A SCHOOL DAY

All the teachers want their students to learn and excel in their studies, thus, they try different methods during a school day. It can be small groups and teamwork, or it can be adding projects with firsthand experiments. However, whatever method is used, the main goal is to get the students interested in the topic and make them to want to learn more on their own.

The School System Comparison Between the United States of America and Finland

The traditional ideas include 'take your child to work' -days when you can take your child to visit your workplace and they can see what it is like to be there.

Or you can present your work at school and tell all the children what it is like to be a police officer or a fireman.

Then the older students can have a month when they work at your workplace just to make them learn what it is like to work there.

Furthermore, the simulation examples include creating a town with small businesses, banks, and then some children are shoppers, some work behind the desk and take orders and money, and some are bankers. The real-life experiments make the children to learn how the economy works, and some businesses sell, some buy, and some are just part of the production chain. Being part of this kind of experiment, makes the children understand the bigger picture.

Also, it allows them to understand the value of money, and what you can buy. The children who pretend to be shopkeepers, learn how to do the inventory in a store and count money. These are all valuable skills.

The money used in these experiments is not real money, but just play money like in a Monopoly game.

CHAPTER 13: MATHEMATICS – INNOVATIVE LEARNING METHODS

In mathematics, the recent trend in Finland is to do the flipping or flipped classroom[1] meaning the students learn by themselves at home.

This means, that if the students have trouble learning at home, then the teacher will assist them, but otherwise, the school time will concentrate on counting.

This allows more time for the teacher to help the students and have one-on-one time, than in the traditional model where the teacher always presents the new topic in front of the classroom.

And the more challenging topics can be reviewed with a group or with the whole classroom. This still lets the teacher to proceed faster and allows the students to proceed on their own pace.

Furthermore, this allows fits well with the e-learning in which the programs allow immediate answer right or wrong, and the students know if they have understood the problem and the solution correctly or not.

The School System Comparison Between the United States of America and Finland

Moreover, this flipped method allows the students proceed further and faster if the teacher allows that.

Thus, the class level limitations no longer apply to a student, if he wants to proceed faster, and he can use the e-learning programs to make sure he grasps the content and topic and follows the requirement s of what is needed to learn in each level at school.

References

1 Tucker, Bill. 2012. "The Flipped Classroom". Education next 12 (1). Retrieved 10/27/2021 from educationnext.org/files/ednext_20121_BTucker.pdf.

CHAPTER 14: LANGUAGE LEARNING INNOVATIVE METHODS

There are many eLearning programs to help with the language learning at schools. Many go through the basic words, and the student just need to pick up which word does not belong to the group.

These have some merits, but eventually, the usability of these programs run out.

More game-like programs keep the students more occupied and interested.

The School System Comparison Between the United States of America and Finland

One of these is Memrise. [1]

It offers clues how to remember a word, and how to pronounce the words. It uses flowers as examples. First, you plant a flower, then feed it and give it water, and then it is time to pick it up. The last phase is when the word is memorized. It also has useful blogs to make the students understand for example Japanese and how to visualize and draw own symbols to make the learning happen.

This app has also useful blogs of different languages, and what language would be useful to learn.

However, many of these language apps require the chance to discuss with the language. Also, they lack the learning and understanding the proper grammar. Thus, that's still part of the curriculum for a language teacher to teach.

In addition, the students do not write their own text with the learned language, and that's still part of what the students need to learn in the classroom with a teacher.

The School System Comparison Between the United States of America and Finland

References

1 Memrise, retrieved 10/21/2021 from www.memrise.com/blog/japanese-kanji-a-memrise-guide

CHAPTER 15: E-LEARNING: STUDENTS VS. TEACHERS

The students nowadays are the generation who is used to use the computers and mobile phones in their daily communications. They are more apt to using any new apps than the teachers, which can be a challenge for a classroom, especially if the classes require e-learning and using new and different programs.

The School System Comparison Between the United States of America and Finland

The teachers could try sometimes to be students in their class. Let the students, or one of them, be the teacher, and teach how to use the apps.

The teachers might find it inspiring to have a student teaching him, and it might excite the students to learn and to discuss about the topic in the classroom.

The subject does not have to be technology, it can be anything that the student is enthusiastic about or even an expert.

This flipping the roles experiment, might promote the atmosphere in the classroom, and make the students more apt to learn more.

In addition, the teachers' time is limited, and any e-learning solution need to be simple and easy to learn in a short period of time.

Moreover, the online gaming programs might also give a different solution for teachers and students to learn. They are easy to use at home, and students can learn and play at home instead of using their school time in learning something trivial.

CHAPTER 16: GLOBAL PANDEMIC AND LEARNING CHALLENGES

The Covid19-pandemic caused rapid, new challenges for schools. The online teaching had to be done in a fast pace, and there was no guarantee, that all the students learn when they try to learn at home instead of at school.

The pandemic made it possible to use administrative programs like Zoom to have group meetings, and teacher-student face-to-face time online.

The e-learning environment also allowed to deliver school materials, and homework online.

In the United States, there was a recent study about the differences of learning based on the socioeconomic background and how the learning disparities will develop during and after the pandemic. This survey study[1] was made in November 2020, and its results are summarized next.

Researchers participated in this study were almost unanimous in their predictions that learning gaps will increase during the covid19 pandemic compared to the time before. In addition, nearly

The School System Comparison Between the United States of America and Finland

half of the respondents believed the growth of learning gaps will fold in 2022, but the rest of the respondents predicted the learning gap will either remain the same or even increase during the year 2022.

Moreover, another study[2] researched the sleeping problems and changes in students' sleep rhythm. The distance learning has affected not just the learning process and methods, but also the sleeping patterns.

This second study found out that if the distant learning is not available daily, the student will go to bed later, and thus the sleep schedule changes based on the availability of the online studies and times.

As a summary, in Finland, the government publishes monthly reports of the different areas of where the global pandemic has affected the different areas of life. One of these is of course the school and learning. The report follows different countries and their research on learning and what problems, disparities, and challenges as well as solutions the different administrations have found.

This report assists in fine-tuning the learning efforts and keeping an eye on the topics that other countries have found out to be challenging.

References

1. Bailey, D.H. et al. (2021) Achievement gaps in the wake of COVID-19. Educational Researcher 50(5): 266-275 (June 2021, first published online April 22, 2021).

2 Meltzer, L.J. et al. (2021) COVID-19 instructional approaches (in-person, online, hybrid), school start times, and sleep in over 5,000 U.S. adolescents. Sleep (Published 17 August 2021).

CHAPTER 17: CONCLUSIONS

There are many similarities in these school systems. Too much homogenizing the education and teaching is a problem in the United States. If you want to encourage individualism, creativity, entrepreneurship, then assessing all the schools and teaching with the same measurements every year, is not the right approach. Some level of creativity and different teaching approaches, methods, and experiments should be allowed if the education aims to the similar level of knowledge.

The School System Comparison Between the United States of America and Finland

Different schools operate in different societies, there might be methods to encourage the students to learn more and to study more if the teachers are given more possibilities to design their classes without considering passing the state-level assessment tests every year.

Including the surrounding society and the culture, backgrounds to teaching are important. The United States is a melting pot of different cultures, and that should be strength in schools and be encouraged also in teaching.

The United States is also seen as a country of innovations and entrepreneurs – this view should be embraced at schools. The creativity is encouraged in America's school system in art and drama classes. I would have loved to have all these kind of classes at school.

These kinds of classes offer you more chances to experience your own creativity, talents, and possibilities to create a career based on your talents. However, I do not see this same level of possibilities to hone your business-, chemistry, physics, or mathematics knowledge.

In summary, there are lots of possibilities to improve the school system, especially if you consider the new technology and use that in teaching and allow students to be more creative with technology.

The School System Comparison Between the United States of America and Finland

Online classes would be a great way to teach some special subjects or even ask the students to return their homework online.

All students reporting – grades and absence – were already online and accessible by parents whenever they wanted.

The future school will allow students to return their homework and projects online and have more flexibility in subjects and school hours. Snow day school hours could be done online easily.

Also, I would encourage the American schools to consider the importance of school lunch and consider the lunch as part of the education that the schools can offer.

In summary, there are not so many differences in subject being taught in these two countries.

More attention should be paid to problem solving and how to use the knowledge in real life situations.

In addition, if the school and the surrounding community can create an environment that supports learning, the results will be better.

Also, if the school can organize small learning groups among students, it will encourage students to learn and to support each other's.

It has been shown that even a poorer community can develop excellent students if the

The School System Comparison Between the United States of America and Finland

students encourage each other and help each other to learn and to go forward in their studies.

When more e-learning methods are introduced to school, the teachers need to have more time to study and learn them, otherwise the students will be more capable than the teachers using the newest technology.

ABOUT THE AUTHOR

The author has a university degree in an AASCB accredited university. She has lived in different states, and currently resides in NY.

The motivation to author this short book was to participate in the current debate in education in the United States.

Milton Keynes UK
Ingram Content Group UK Ltd.
UKHW022332030324
438776UK00014B/2284